# Staying Safe

# Safety at the Playground

By MaryLee Knowlton
Photography by Gregg Andersen

## Crabtree Publishing Company

www.crabtreebooks.com

# Crabtree Publishing Company

## www.crabtreebooks.com

**Author**: MaryLee Knowlton
**Project coordinator:** Robert Walker
**Editor:** Reagan Miller
**Proofreaders:** Molly Aloian, Crystal Sikkens
**Production coordinator:** Katherine Kantor
**Prepress technicians:** Samara Parent, Ken Wright
**Design**: Westgraphix/Tammy West

Written, developed, and produced by
Water Buffalo Books/Mark Sachner Publishing Services

**Photographs**: © Gregg Andersen/Gallery 19

**Acknowledgments**:
The publisher, producer, and photographer
gratefully acknowledge the following people for their
participation in the making of this book:
In Soldotna, Alaska: Dallas Armstrong, Mary Armstrong,
Chris Kempf, Er Kempf, Jackie Kempf, Etta Mae Near,
Jerome Near, Janet O'Toole, Mike O'Toole, John Pothast.
In Mankato, Minnesota: Debbie Benke, Candee Deichman,
Liz Goertzen, Syndie Johnson, Brianna Ostoff. And a special
thanks is offered to the dozens of school children, staff, and
parents who gave generously and enthusiastically of their
time and talent in the making of this book.

Library and Archives Canada Cataloguing in Publication

Knowlton, MaryLee, 1946-
    Safety at the playground / MaryLee Knowlton ; photography
by Gregg Andersen.

(Staying safe)
Includes index.
ISBN 978-0-7787-4318-7 (bound).--ISBN 978-0-7787-4323-1 (pbk.)

    1. Playgrounds--Safety measures--Juvenile literature. 2. Safety
education--Juvenile literature. I. Andersen, Gregg  II. Title.
III. Series: Staying safe (St. Catharines, Ont.)

GV424.K56 2008          j613.6          C2008-905550-0

Library of Congress Cataloging-in-Publication Data

Knowlton, MaryLee, 1946-
    Safety at the playground / by MaryLee Knowlton ; photography by Gregg Andersen.
        p. cm. --  (Staying safe)
    Includes index.
    ISBN-13: 978-0-7787-4323-1 (pbk. : alk. paper)
    ISBN-10: 0-7787-4323-3 (pbk. : alk. paper)
    ISBN-13: 978-0-7787-4318-7 (reinforced library binding : alk. paper)
    ISBN-10: 0-7787-4318-7 (reinforced library binding : alk. paper)
    1. Playgrounds--Safety measures--Juvenile literature. I. Andersen, Gregg, ill. II. Title. III. Series.

GV424.K64 2009
796.06'8--dc22

                                        2008036591

## Crabtree Publishing Company

www.crabtreebooks.com          1-800-387-7650

Printed in the U.S.A./012014/SN20131105

**Published in Canada**
Crabtree Publishing
616 Welland Ave.
St. Catharines, ON
L2M 5V6

**Published in the United States**
Crabtree Publishing
PMB16A
350 Fifth Ave., Suite 3308
New York, NY  10118

**Published in the United Kingdom**
Crabtree Publishing
White Cross Mills
High Town, Lancaster
LA1 4XS

**Published in Australia**
Crabtree Publishing
386 Mt. Alexander Rd.
Ascot Vale (Melbourne)
VIC 3032

# Contents

Words in **bold** are defined in the glossary on page 30.

# Staying Safe at the Playground

Every day, you have to make choices about your own safety. Whether you are at home, at school, around water, or at a playground, staying safe is something you must always think about.

In this book, each section presents a special playground safety **hazard** or problem.

# Here is how the book works:

**First**, you will read about a problem at the playground.

**Second**, you will choose how to solve the problem.

**Third**, you will learn about the **consequence**, or outcome, of each choice.

For every bad consequence, you will see a "no" sign.

For every good consequence, you will see a gold star.

**Finally**, you will learn which is the best choice and why.

You will also learn about ways to play safely when you are away from home at a playground or park. Telling your friends what you learn will help them make safe choices, too!

# Leaving the Playground

Parks and playgrounds have **equipment** and open fields where you can run and play. But sometimes you can see things going on just outside of where you are supposed to be.

What do you do when you want to run over and see something outside of the playground?

# What's happening?

You have come to the playground with your best friend, Dina, and her mother. You see your other friend, Jack, and his new puppy across the street.

## What should you do?

A. Look carefully to see that no cars are coming and run over to see the puppy.

B. Tell Dina to tell her mother that you're going to see the puppy, and off you go.

C. Ask Dina's mother if she'll take you and Dina across the street to see Jack's puppy.

**Which is the best choice?**

**Turn the page** .......... **and find out!**

# What happens next:

## If you choose A ...

Dina and her mother might not know where you are. They could get very worried. 🚫

## If you choose B ...

Dina's mother might tell you that she won't bring you to the park anymore because you left without telling her. 🚫

Dina and her mother come
with you to see the puppy.

**The best choice is C.**
Be sure you talk to Dina's mother and she takes
you across the street.

## What have you learned?

The first rule of the playground is this:
Never go where the adult who brought
you can't see you.

# "No Pushing!"

Sometimes you have to wait a long time for your turn on the playground equipment. Waiting can be hard. Other people have trouble waiting, too.

What should you do when another kid tries to get in line ahead of you?

## What's happening?

Another kid pushes you out of line while you're waiting to climb up the ladder to the slide.

## What should you do?

A. Race up the ladder ahead of him or her.

B. Push him or her right back out of line.

C. Step out of line and find a grownup in charge to help settle things.

**Which is the best choice?**

Turn the page .......... and find out!

# What happens next:

## If you choose A . . .

You might make the other kids angry for not waiting your turn. You could also hurt yourself as you race up the ladder!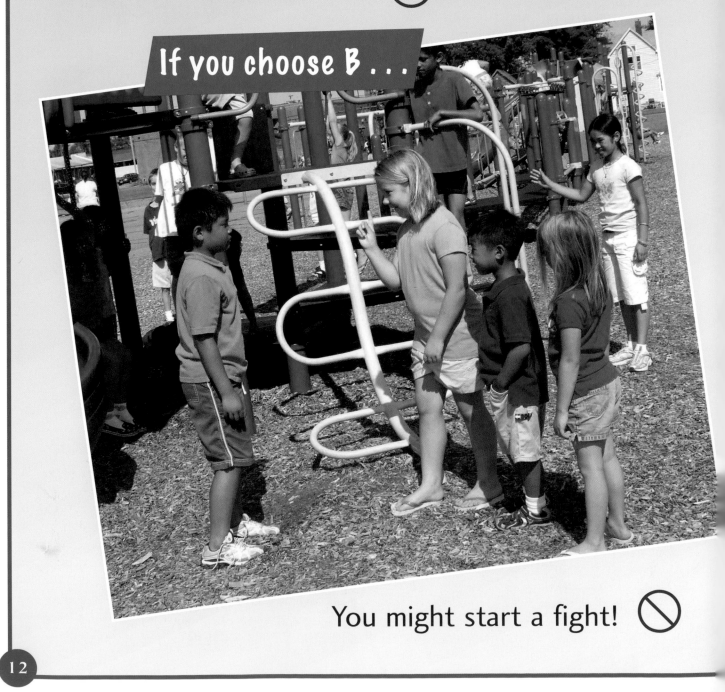

## If you choose B . . .

You might start a fight!

## If you choose C . . .

You will put an end to the pushing and make sure all the kids in line are safe and get a turn.

The best choice is C.
Let a grownup decide where everyone should be in line.

### What have you learned?

Pushing back is never a way to get others to stop pushing. Treat people the way you want them to treat you.

# Throwing Things

The park or playground is a great place to throw balls or Frisbees because there is so much room. You can run far and throw high or long without breaking a window or hitting a car. You must remember, however, that there are other people at the park!

How can you practice your throwing and catching safely?

## What's happening?

You and your brother want to throw a Frisbee while your parents finish eating a picnic lunch.

## What should you do?

A. Go to another area of the park where your parents are out of the way and you are out of their sight.

B. Throw the Frisbee high so it goes over their heads.

C. Wait until the adults finish eating. Then ask one of them to come with you to a place where your throwing and catching won't bother or hurt anyone.

## Which is the best choice?

Turn the page.............→ and find out!

# What happens next:

## If you choose A . . .

Your parents may become worried about you since they don't know where you are playing. You could get in big trouble for breaking the first rule of the playground: Stay where the adults you came with can find you. ⊘

## If you choose B . . .

Your brother could miss a catch and the Frisbee might land in the middle of someone's meal! ⊘

Everybody has fun and gets to enjoy the picnic.

### The best choice is C.

Get a grownup to take you somewhere where you won't disturb anyone with your throwing and catching.

### What have you learned?

Don't throw things where other people are eating or not **expecting** things flying through the air. People can get hurt or you can make a big mess. Always stay where the adults who brought you can see you.

# Picking Things Up

Parks and playgrounds are places where everybody can go to play and have fun. Keep them clean and safe by picking up your own trash and throwing it away where it belongs.

What can you do when people leave trash lying around and other kids get into it?

# What's happening?

You're at the playground and it's a mess. Someone has left trash all over the place and your little brother is digging around in it.

## What should you do?

**A.** Pick up the trash and throw it in a container.

**B.** Tell your brother to leave the trash alone.

**C.** Tell the adult who brought you to the park. He or she can decide whether to tell a park employee about it or take you somewhere else to play.

## Which is the best choice?

Turn the page and find out!

# What happens next:

## If you choose A . . .

You might touch germs or **molds** that have grown on the trash. These can make you sick. ⊘

## If you choose B . . .

Your brother won't do what you say for long. He might get cut on a piece of glass—or eat a hot dog he found in the dirt! ⊘

20

You see that trash can be dangerous. You have done the right thing by telling an adult about it.

### The best choice is C.

Talk about the trash to the grownup who brought you. He or she can figure out the best way to take care of it. Cleaning up other people's garbage is not your responsibility!

## What have you learned?

Some people who come to the park don't clean up after themselves, even though you always do. It is not your job to clean up after other people in a **public** place. You can get hurt picking up other people's trash.

# Talking to Strangers

Most of the people in the park or on the playground have come there to have a good time, just like you. But you can't be sure if you don't know them. That's one reason you always come with an adult.

What should you do if someone you don't know asks you to go with him or her?

# What's happening?

A man comes up to you and your sister and shows you a picture of his puppy. He tells you it's lost and asks you to help find it.

## What should you do?

**A.** You and your sister both go with the man to help him find the puppy because the two of you can watch each other.

**B.** You ask your sister to tell your mom that you're helping a man find his puppy, so your mom will know where you are.

**C.** You and your sister don't talk to the man. Instead, you go to your mom and tell her a stranger asked you to go with him.

### Which is the best choice?

Turn the page·········→ and find out!

# What happens next:

## If you choose A . . .

There is no puppy. The man might pull both your sister and you into his car as soon as you are out of your mother's sight. 🚫

## If you choose B . . .

The man has tricked you into coming with him. He might pull you into his car as soon as your sister is out of sight. 🚫

Your mother tells the police
that a stranger is bothering children
in the park. You and your sister are safe.

## The best choice is C.
You leave it up to your mom to figure out
what to do about the stranger.

## what have you learned?
Never go with a stranger or let him or
her give you anything. Never go anywhere
without telling the person who takes care of you.
You don't have to figure out whether you can trust
a stranger. That is an adult's job, not yours!

# Petting Animals

Many people come to the park to walk their dogs. Some people do not keep their dogs on leashes.

What should you do when you see a cute puppy or a friendly looking dog?

# What's happening?

Some people in the park are playing Frisbee with their dog. The Frisbee lands near you. The dog comes running over to you with its tail wagging. You really love dogs, and you want to pet it.

## What should you do?

A. Pick up the Frisbee and say, "Here boy! Here Boy!" and throw your arms around the dog.

B. Pick up the Frisbee and throw it back to the people who threw it.

C. Stand still and leave the Frisbee and the dog alone.

## Which is the best choice?

Turn the page and find out!

# What happens next:

## If you choose A . . .

The dog is frightened by being handled by someone it doesn't know. It might bite you.

## If you choose B . . .

The dog becomes confused because someone it doesn't know took its Frisbee while it was chasing it. The dog could bite you.

## If you choose C . . .

You don't frighten the dog and it doesn't bite anyone. The owners of the dog can come over, get the Frisbee, and be sure their dog behaves itself.

### The best choice is C.

It's not your job to fetch the Frisbee and return it to the dog's owners. Your main responsibility is to keep yourself safe!

### What have you learned?

Most people's pets are friendly, but you don't know that for sure. Never touch an animal unless its owner is there and tells you it's ok. Even though you are very nice, some animals are afraid of people.

Did you know that some dogs work to keep people safe? Some dogs are trained for jobs like helping their owners cross the street or checking to be sure packages are safe. Some even work with firefighters or police to help find people who are lost. Dogs that are trained to do jobs are called **service dogs**. Petting them while they're working keeps them from doing their job.

# Glossary

**consequence** The result or effect of an action; a thing that happens as a result of something else happening

**employee** A person who is paid to work for someone else

**equipment** Anything that is provided for use, such as swings or slides on a playground

**expecting** Thinking that something will happen; being ready for something to happen

**hazard** A danger or a chance to get hurt

**molds** An often fuzzy, plantlike growth that appears on damp or rotting matter

**public** Open to or shared by many people; out in the open

**service dogs** Dogs that are specially trained to help people who are very old or have disabilities

**stranger** A person who is new to an area or unknown to others

## BOOKS

*Play It Smart: Playground Safety* (How to Be Safe!). Jill Donahue. Picture Window Books, 2008.

*Please Play Safe! Penguin's Guide to Playground Safety.* Margery Cuyler. Scholastic, 2006.

## WEBSITES

**The Further Adventures of Kidd Safety**
http://www.cpsc.gov/kids/kidsafety/
From bicycle safety to helping adults figure out how to make playground equipment safe, this site provides tips, posters, and safety lists for kids and grownups alike.

**Kids.gov: The Official Kids' Portal for the U.S. Government**
http://www.kids.gov/k_5/k_5_health_safety.shtml
This site provides information and activities that teach and encourage safety. It also includes an amazing list of links to other sites about safety everywhere—including at playgrounds, in traffic, and around strangers.

**McGruff.org**
http://www.mcgruff.org/
Kids learn how to stop a bully with games, trading cards, Internet posters, and stories.

**Playground Safety for Kids!**
http://www.kidchecker.org/story.htm
From safety tips to becoming a kid checker and offering ways to help, this site is run by two kids who tell others how to be sure their playground is safe.

# Index